Poems & Songs

by an "old" hippie

S0-BNQ-397

Carl Faulhaber

published by

Peanut Butter Publishing
Seattle, Washington
Portland, Oregon
Denver, Colorado
Vancouver, B.C.

ISBN # 0-89716-750-3
LC # 97-
B0.S047

Typesetting by Packard Productions

First printing April 1997
10 9 8 7 6 5 4 3 2 1

Printed in the United States of America

Peanut Butter Publishing
226 Second Avenue West, Seattle, WA 98119
Old Post Office Bldg., 510 SW Third
Portland, OR 97201
Cherry Creek, 50 S. Steele, Suite 850
Denver, CO 80209
Ste. 230 1333 Johnston Street, Pier 32,
Granville Island, Vancouver, BC V6H 3 R9
e mail: pnutpub@aol.com
Internet: http://www.pbpublishing.com

Dedication

This book is dedicated to
Kristel and Kyle: my two beautiful
children
who make it all worthwhile.

Notes from the Author:

I didn't keep good records
when the poems and songs were written.
I know they were written during the period
from the late 60s to the early 70s.
When I first thought about putting together
this book,
I thought it would be good to add some
history to each poem and song
so people would know how it came to be.
Then I thought, if you were part of that era
you would have your own stories
that would fit. I'm sure your stories would
make more sense to you
than what I could write. If you weren't part
of that era or didn't indulge, don't worry.
The poems and songs apply to you as well.
I know some people won't agree with this but,
it was a time of innocence.
And, just like all times of innocence,
they must come to an end
to make room for new ones.
Peace

Carl Faulhaber
December 1996

Table of Contents

Plastic People

In this world of men and women
When life just isn't worth living.
And people crowd you from all sides,
Then you're the one who needs a guide.
People staring you in the eye
Trying to see if you don't lie.
Don't be yourself, you have to conform.
Then they try to tell you weren't even born.
If this my friend is happening to you
And you don't know where to run
      or what to do.
Then take these plastic people
Take them by the hand.
Twist them, bend them, it's your turn
      to take a stand.
Tell them that you want to be
Not a pig but, someone free.
To live in a world of peace and love
Where nobody is below, no one above.
Where people can walk hand in hand
And there is harmony, not hate over this land.
Yes my brothers and sisters I would do this
For the plastic people cannot persist.
For they have no real convictions, no real mind.
This is why you should strike them blind.
You have to be free,
      To live like you want to be.

(November 1969)

October 15
(Vietnam War Moratorium)

OCT. 15:   *A day to remember,*
OCT. 15:   *A day to see.*
OCT. 15:   *When people will say,*
OCT. 15:   *End the war today.*

OCT. 15:   *The war is long,*
OCT. 15:   *Dissent is strong,*
OCT. 15:   *The people have said,*
OCT. 15:   *There are enough dead.*

OCT. 15:   *When young and old,*
OCT. 15:   *Will unite as one.*
OCT. 15:   *And begin to yell,*
OCT. 15:   *Enough of this hell.*

OCT. 15:   *Will they hear?*
OCT. 15:   *That we are sincere.*
OCT. 15:   *Will they listen?*
OCTOBER FIFTEEN

(October 15, 1969)

3

Stoned

Clouds in the sky
    I just want to die.
Hair in my eyes
    Does nobody lie?

Music in the air
    People like to stare.
Look at the funny glare
    Is it too much to bare?

Birds in flight
    It's quite a site.
My pants feel tight
    You want to fly a kite?

The air outside
    I need a guide.
Somebody lied
    My bird just died.

The winds blowing
    My mom's sewing.
The farmer's hoeing
    Where am I going?

(March 1970)

♪ One Unanswered Question ♪

I wake up in the morning light,
The sparkling dew is glistening
    on the leaves.
I know the time to say good-bye
    has shadowed us but, we must part.
But how can I leave you now,
    I love you so I can't let go.

I look into your eyes and see the tears
    you try to hide.
I try to tell you not to cry but,
    the words are hard to find.
You hold my hand and squeeze it,
    thoughts of love begin to grow.
And all the times that we had,
    it's hard to say that I won't cry.

Refrain: You ask me when I will return,
    I don't know, it's hard to say.
    I've never felt this way inside,
    I want you more
        each minute we stay,
            But I must go.

I touch your face so gently, my lips
    touch yours and yours to mine.
So softly and so sweetly,
    a kiss I wish would never stop.

7

Your body is so close to mine,
  I feel the beat of a lonely heart.

Refrain: *You ask me when I will return,*
  I don't know, it's hard to say.
  I've never felt this way inside,
  I want you more each minute
    we stay,
      But I must go.

All the dreams that we both had,
  they slowly creep into the haze.
So now the end has finally come,
  I start to walk out the door.
You grab my hand, I turn around,
  you say to me, love is strong.
I bow my head, I stare at the ground,
  I whisper softly, "War is long,"

(August 1970)

Fleeting Moments

There once was a boy
  who was lost in the woods.

He hopelessly walked
  in many directions but,

He couldn't find his way.

Then one day he met a girl
  who gave him new life.

Happiness was his for a half and one year.

Suddenly, the girl disappeared.

There once was a boy
  who was lost in the woods.

(December 1970)

♪ Stainglass Window ♪

As I look out my stainglass window,
I saw a man who walked alone.
His eyes did not wander but straight ahead,
Deaf to the world was this gentleman.

Chorus:
But we know what's wrong, don't we?

As I look out my stainglass window,
pretty ladies walked slowly by.
White was the color of their hapless faces,
No handsome man could move their eyes.

Chorus:
But we know what's wrong, don't we?

As I look out my stainglass window,
Little children, what sorry souls.
Cause they no longer laugh and shout,
Nor smile and romp about.

Chorus:
But we know what's wrong, don't we?

As I look out my stainglass window,
I saw a baby who cried so loud.
Too young to understand,
No bottle to comfort him.

Chorus:
But we know what's wrong, don't we?

As we look out our stainglass window,
We see a dove fall from the sky.
Is that why the people are frightened?
Is it too late to reason why?

(January 1971)

What's Wrong With The Mind The Way It Is?

Search your soul, read your mind,
Find the light, carry the load.
I know it's hard, yes, I know.
I know that people need something to do,
But I can't see your point of view.
Are you listening, am I getting through?

Chorus:
But, what's wrong with the mind
  the way it is?

Search your soul, read your mind,
Find the light, carry the load.
Don't turn your back to me.
I see your eyes point to the sky,
Is that what you call a high?
Are you sure you're not messin' yourself?

Chorus:
But, what's wrong with the mind
  the way it is?

(Oohs)

Find a corner, see if you can hide.
Why not turn back now,
    before you end up dead?
Real life is hard I know,
    the problems today are out of control.
Together we can make it through
To help each other is what we'll do.

Chorus:
But, what's wrong with the mind
    the way it is?

(February 1971)

I Cry For You

I remember days gone by,
    when the sun was shining high.
When the birds were singing loud,
    when I smiled and not frowned.
I used to laugh and shout,
    you were the one I talked about.
Your face would show of love,
    like the beauty of a white dove.

Chorus: And now the rain begins to fall,
       My thoughts are washed
          into the ground.
       Will I ever see the morning sun?
       I cry for you.

I see you in my dreams,
    I feel your body close to mine.
When I was near to you,
    angels I heard inside.
Little things you did for me,
    made me feel so proud.
Because I was the one,
    it was a world without end.

Chorus: And now the rain begins to fall,
       My thoughts are washed
          into the ground.
       Will I ever see the morning sun?
       I cry for you.

Refrain: We used to go to the sea,
We would play in the sand.
The castles we built I thought
   were strong,
But now they come tumbling down.

Chorus: And now the rain begins to fall,
My thoughts are washed
   into the ground.
Will I ever see the morning sun?
I cry for you.

(February 1971)

Random Thoughts

The wind blows fiercely outside.

The curtains sway to an offbeat rhythm.

Leaves strain to keep to their limbs.

Two people, friends indeed,
*   snore a happy snore.*

The tick of the clock warns of tomorrow.

A new life, a brand new ball game.

So, here I sit.

(August 1971, first night in a
new apartment with two friends)

♪ *Reminders* ♪

Dance through a meadow of green grass,
Throw stones across a clear, blue lake.
Listen to birds sing their happy
  songs of life.

Chorus: *All these simple signs show*
  what you mean to me.

Watch the clouds on your back
  in knee deep grass,
Spin around in a crooked circle
  and fall to the ground.
Play with a child who doesn't
  know your name.

Chorus: *All these simple signs show*
  what you mean to me.

Look over the hill to a house
  of white brick,
  a baby cries.
Its mother comes to comfort,
  she knows not why.
The baby smiles and mother knows.

Chorus: *All these simple signs show*
  what you mean to me.

Blonde hair blowing free
*   in the soft summer air.*
One hold of your hand takes me
*   to another world.*
A smile, a kiss, a sigh.

Chorus: *All these simple signs show*
*   what you mean to me.*

(August 1971)

?Why

? Why did I get up this morning

? Why did the sun rise

? Why did I go to church

? Why did I give money

? Why did I eat three times

? Why did I open doors

? Why did I close them

? Why did I go to work

? Why did the sun set

? Why did I go to sleep

? Why did I write this

(date unknown)

♪ That's The Way It Was ♪

Let's pretend we are in a dream,
Where all good things happen.
Only happiness is supreme.
And let's pretend the trees are golden.
The night is cold,
And it's just you and me.
The silence around is forbidding.
To many only a pure fantasy.
And the stars twinkle bright in the heavens.
You kiss me soft,
No words can fit the scene.

Chorus: That's the way it was,
    the first night I met you.
Like a flower blossoming
    in the spring,
You gave me a reason to sing.
A dream that did come true but,
Now you're gone, what can I do?

Sometimes I wonder if it's just all there.
Am I kidding myself,
    how do I know you really care?
Then I stop and think of the fun we had,
    little I know but,

It was enough to make me see,
How much you think and care about me.

Chorus: That's the way it was,
   the first night I met you.
Like a flower blossoming
   in the spring,
You gave me a reason to sing.
A dream that did come true but,
Now you're gone, what can I do?

Now I know what must be done,
Somehow it's like the rising sun.
Every new day that it brings,
With the birds, oh how they sing.
Everyday I will think of you.
In the morning when the sky is blue,
In the evening when I go to sleep.
A dream like this is hard to keep.

Chorus: That's the way it was,
   the first night I met you.
Like a flower blossoming
   in the spring,
You gave me a reason to sing.
A dream that did come true but,
Now you're gone, what can I do?

(date unknown)

Answers Without

Can't stop thinking, if it's just all worth it.
Just can't seem to think straight.

Many things are done,
*   some things left undone.*
Confusion sets in too often.

Being young and being free.
Ready to conquer, scared to fall.

Trying to be heard in a world of shadows.
Listening to criticism, none too good.

Not talking back, only wasted words.
Turned heads everywhere,
*   not one helping hand.*

Why aren't the answers
**   in the back of the book?**

(date unknown)

Together

When summer's had its final fling

And the birds stop flying
   and no more sing.

Then will I think of the day you left

And how that last kiss was so short.

But how it reminded me of the first

And the feelings I had that cold,
   crisp night.

(Now that you're gone) the feelings
   I had are still there,

But now they're stronger
   with each passing day.

And now I hope when I again
   can touch your hand,

When I can kiss your lips
   and see you smile.

That you will be there,
   mind and body, with mine.

United, to face those uncertain days---
   Together.

(date unknown)

39

Promises

I can't promise you the world

For that is not mine to give.

I can't promise you happiness,

Only you can make it happen.

I can't promise you tomorrow

For today is all I know.

I can't promise you the moon and the stars

For they are for everyone.

But I can promise me

For that is the only possession I have.

And with that I hope

Will you accept

And be content.

(date unknown)

41

Silhouette on the Road

Thumb pointed with a questioned
    confidence,

Face red, wind is not a friend.

Man against machine, nature a spectator.

All alone on a black floor,
    the stars are his only companions.

The moon gives off a sinister smile,

To hide from it is only for fools.

A comet streaks across the sky.

A wish is made but, no reply.

        *(date unknown, written for a hitchhiker
        poster drawn by a friend.)*

♪ Title Unknown ♪

Morning to night I hear people say,
About how the world is splitting apart.
How the young people have gone astray.
How the leaders of our nation
    don't speak for us.
And yet after all I've heard,
The answers were never found.
Just wasted words that mean nothing.
But if I could give a message
    for all the world to hear,
I'd tell them,

Chorus: *Try to smile a little each day,*
        Help a friend out when you can.
        Don't look back on what has been,
        Face the new day
            when the sun shines in.

Yes, these words will go unheeded,
Unless people can sit and talk
    and respect each side.
Until you and I can walk peacefully
    in this beautiful world of ours.
I don't know if I'll ever see it happen
    in my lifetime but,
If I can do just one good deed for mankind,

I can die knowing that I strived to make it
  come to be but,
While I'm alive I'm going to,

Chorus: *Try to smile a little each day,*
   Help a friend out when you can.
   Don't look back on what has been,
   Face the new day
    when the sun shines in.

       (date unknown)

♪ My Life ♪

My life so far has been complete,
With all my friends, I love, I'll keep.
With everyday that comes along.
I can't help thinking what a life I've found.

I've been here, I've been there,
I've had a lot of moments to share.
But isn't that what life's all about?
It's all mine, it makes me want to shout.

Refrain: I'm gonna live until I die,
Sometimes I'll wonder why.
I'm gonna sing what must be sung,
I'm gonna love what's in my heart.

I think of tomorrow and what it may bring.
Yesterday is over, today I begin,
To make my life and the world around,
A little bit happier so love will abound.

Refrain: I'm gonna live until I die,
Sometimes I'll wonder why.
I'm gonna sing what must be sung,
I'm gonna love what's in my heart.

But now I have just one thing to say,
To all you people who made this day.
With you in my life I'll always be high,
My life thanks you, so do I.

(date unknown)

Final Thoughts:

*I hope you enjoyed this brief interlude
into my past.
I enjoyed sharing it with you.
Now, I want to get some feedback from
you.
I have some thoughts and ideas about
future editions.
I want to have an edition for the blind.
Some folks say I should
add the music
that goes with the songs. Others think
it would be cool to add art
and photographs
from the era.
Others say it would be good
to have a "coffee table" book format
with larger print
for us aging boomers.
They're all great ideas. What do you
think??
If you are so inclined,
let me know what's on your mind.
Here's how you can let me know:*

**Carl Faulhaber
191 University Blvd. #381
Denver, CO 80206
(303) 722.9914
1.888.282.7873
Email: carlf@usa.net**